EMMANUEL JOSEPH

Play to Learn, Learn to Live, The Intersection of Gaming, Education, and Spirituality

Copyright © 2025 by Emmanuel Joseph

All rights reserved. No part of this publication may be reproduced, stored or transmitted in any form or by any means, electronic, mechanical, photocopying, recording, scanning, or otherwise without written permission from the publisher. It is illegal to copy this book, post it to a website, or distribute it by any other means without permission.

First edition

This book was professionally typeset on Reedsy.
Find out more at reedsy.com

Contents

1	Chapter 1: The Role of Play in Human Development	1
2	Chapter 2: The Evolution of Gaming	3
3	Chapter 3: Gamification in Education	5
4	Chapter 4: The Spiritual Dimension of Play	7
5	Chapter 5: Educational Video Games	9
6	Chapter 6: The Psychology of Gaming	11
7	Chapter 7: The Benefits of Play for Adults	13
8	Chapter 8: Educational Benefits of Gaming	15
9	Chapter 9: The Spirituality of Gaming	17
10	Chapter 10: Playful Learning in the Classroom	19
11	Chapter 11: The Future of Gaming in Education	21
12	Chapter 12: Embracing Play in Our Lives	23
13	Chapter 13: Balancing Play and Work	25
14	Chapter 14: Play and Emotional Intelligence	27
15	Chapter 15: The Intersection of Gaming, Education, and...	29

1

Chapter 1: The Role of Play in Human Development

P lay is an intrinsic part of human development, dating back to our earliest ancestors. It serves as a means of exploration, problem-solving, and social interaction. Children engage in play to learn about their environment, develop cognitive skills, and build relationships with others. Play is not just a frivolous activity; it is a fundamental aspect of growth and learning. As we grow older, the nature of play may change, but its importance remains.

In the realm of education, play-based learning has gained recognition for its effectiveness in fostering creativity and critical thinking. Through play, students can engage with complex concepts in a hands-on and meaningful way. Games and playful activities can make learning more enjoyable and memorable, encouraging students to take an active role in their education. By incorporating play into the classroom, educators can create a dynamic and engaging learning environment.

The benefits of play extend beyond the classroom. In our daily lives, play can serve as a form of relaxation and stress relief. Engaging in recreational activities allows us to unwind and recharge, promoting mental and emotional well-being. Play can also foster social connections, as it often involves interaction with others. Whether it's a friendly game of soccer or a board game with family and friends, play brings people together and strengthens relationships.

Moreover, play has a spiritual dimension. It can be a way of experiencing joy, wonder, and a sense of connection to something greater than ourselves. Many spiritual traditions incorporate play and ritual to foster a sense of community and transcendence. By embracing play in all its forms, we can enrich our lives and deepen our understanding of ourselves and the world around us.

2

Chapter 2: The Evolution of Gaming

The history of gaming is a testament to the enduring human fascination with play. From ancient board games to the latest video games, gaming has evolved to reflect cultural, technological, and social changes. Early games like Senet in ancient Egypt and Go in ancient China were not just pastimes but also held religious and philosophical significance. These games required strategic thinking and provided a way for people to connect with each other and their beliefs.

The advent of digital technology brought about a revolution in gaming. The creation of arcade games in the 1970s, such as Pong and Space Invaders, marked the beginning of a new era. These games captivated players with their simple yet addictive gameplay. As technology advanced, so did the complexity and realism of video games. The introduction of home gaming consoles in the 1980s and 1990s made gaming accessible to a wider audience, leading to the rise of iconic games like Super Mario and The Legend of Zelda.

In the 21st century, gaming has become a global phenomenon. Online multiplayer games like World of Warcraft and Fortnite have created virtual worlds where players can interact and compete with others from around the world. The rise of esports has turned gaming into a spectator sport, with professional players and teams competing for large prizes. Gaming has also become a platform for storytelling, with games like The Last of Us and Red Dead Redemption offering rich narratives and immersive experiences.

Despite its evolution, the essence of gaming remains the same: it is a form of play that challenges our minds and provides a sense of accomplishment. Games can transport us to different worlds, allow us to experiment with different identities, and offer a space for creativity and self-expression. As gaming continues to evolve, it will undoubtedly remain a vital part of human culture and an important tool for education and personal growth.

3

Chapter 3: Gamification in Education

Gamification is the application of game design elements in non-game contexts, such as education. This approach leverages the motivational aspects of games to enhance learning experiences. By incorporating elements like points, badges, and leaderboards, educators can create a more engaging and interactive learning environment. Gamification has been shown to increase student motivation, participation, and retention of information.

One of the key benefits of gamification is its ability to make learning more fun and enjoyable. Traditional education methods can sometimes be monotonous and disengaging. Gamification introduces an element of excitement and competition, making learning feel more like a game. This can be particularly effective for younger students, who are naturally drawn to play and exploration.

Gamification also promotes active learning. Instead of passively receiving information, students are encouraged to take an active role in their education. They can solve problems, complete challenges, and make decisions that impact their learning outcomes. This hands-on approach helps students develop critical thinking and problem-solving skills. It also fosters a sense of ownership and responsibility for their learning.

Furthermore, gamification can provide immediate feedback and recognition. In traditional education, students may have to wait for days or weeks to receive feedback on their work. In a gamified environment, they can receive instant feedback, allowing them to learn from their mistakes and improve. Recognition in the form of badges or rewards can also boost student confidence and motivation. By gamifying education, we can create a more dynamic and effective learning experience.

4

Chapter 4: The Spiritual Dimension of Play

Play is not only a physical and mental activity but also has a spiritual dimension. Many spiritual traditions recognize the importance of play as a way to connect with the divine, explore one's inner self, and experience a sense of transcendence. Through play, we can tap into a deeper level of consciousness and gain insights into our spiritual nature.

In some cultures, play is integrated into religious rituals and ceremonies. For example, Native American tribes incorporate games and dances into their spiritual practices to honor their gods and ancestors. These activities are seen as a way to connect with the spiritual realm and seek guidance and blessings. Similarly, in Hinduism, the festival of Holi involves playful activities like throwing colored powder, which symbolize the joy and vibrancy of life.

Play can also be a form of meditation. Activities like yoga, tai chi, and mindful movement combine physical play with a focus on mindfulness and inner awareness. These practices help individuals cultivate a sense of peace, balance, and connection to the present moment. By engaging in such playful activities, we can experience a deeper sense of spirituality and well-being.

Moreover, play can foster a sense of community and belonging, which is an important aspect of spiritual growth. Participating in group activities, whether it's a team sport or a cooperative game, allows us to connect with others on a deeper level. Through play, we can build relationships, develop empathy, and experience a sense of unity. This sense of connection is a key component of many spiritual traditions, which emphasize the importance of community and shared experiences.

5

Chapter 5: Educational Video Games

Video games have the potential to be powerful educational tools. By combining engaging gameplay with educational content, video games can create immersive learning experiences. Educational video games can cover a wide range of subjects, from mathematics and science to history and language arts. These games can make learning more interactive and enjoyable, helping students develop important skills and knowledge.

One of the advantages of educational video games is their ability to provide personalized learning experiences. Unlike traditional classroom settings, video games can adapt to the individual needs and abilities of each student. They can offer different levels of difficulty, provide hints and feedback, and track progress. This personalized approach allows students to learn at their own pace and receive targeted support.

Educational video games can also promote critical thinking and problem-solving skills. Many games require players to analyze information, make decisions, and solve complex problems. These cognitive skills are essential for academic success and lifelong learning. By engaging with educational video games, students can develop these skills in a fun and engaging way.

Furthermore, video games can enhance collaboration and communication. Many educational games include multiplayer or cooperative modes, where students can work together to achieve common goals. This encourages teamwork, communication, and social interaction. By playing these games, students can develop important social skills and learn how to work effectively with others.

6

Chapter 6: The Psychology of Gaming

The psychology of gaming explores how games impact our thoughts, feelings, and behaviors. Games have a unique ability to engage and captivate players, creating a state of flow where they are fully immersed and focused. This state of flow is associated with increased enjoyment, motivation, and performance. Understanding the psychological aspects of gaming can help us harness its potential for positive impact.

One of the key psychological elements of gaming is motivation. Games are designed to be rewarding, providing players with a sense of achievement and progress. This is often achieved through the use of rewards, challenges, and feedback. By understanding what motivates players, game designers can create experiences that are both enjoyable and educational.

Games also have the power to influence our emotions. They can evoke a wide range of feelings, from excitement and joy to frustration and empathy. By tapping into our emotions, games can create memorable and impactful experiences. This emotional engagement can enhance learning and retention of information, making games a valuable tool for education and personal growth.

Moreover, games can promote social interaction and connection. Multiplayer games, in particular, provide opportunities for players to collaborate, compete, and communicate with others. This social aspect of gaming can foster a sense of community and belonging. It can also help players develop important social skills, such as teamwork, communication, and empathy.

7

Chapter 7: The Benefits of Play for Adults

Play is often associated with children, but its benefits extend to adults as well. Engaging in play can promote mental, emotional, and physical well-being. It provides a break from the stresses of daily life, allowing adults to relax and recharge. Play can also foster creativity, problem-solving, and social connections, making it an important aspect of a healthy and fulfilling life.

One of the benefits of play for adults is stress relief. Life can be demanding, and taking time to engage in playful activities can provide a much-needed escape. Whether it's playing a sport, participating in a hobby, or enjoying a game with friends, play allows adults to unwind and have fun.

This can reduce stress levels and improve overall mental health. Engaging in play also promotes physical health. Activities like sports, dancing, and outdoor games provide exercise, helping to maintain physical fitness and reduce the risk of chronic diseases. Moreover, playful activities can stimulate the brain, keeping it active and sharp. This can improve cognitive functions such as memory, concentration, and problem-solving skills.

Creativity is another significant benefit of play for adults. Play encourages imaginative thinking and innovation. Whether it's through artistic endeavors, like painting or writing, or more structured activities, like building with LEGO bricks or solving puzzles, play allows adults to explore new ideas and think outside the box. This creative thinking can have practical applications in the workplace and personal projects.

Social connections are also enhanced through play. Participating in games and recreational activities with others fosters social interaction and strengthens relationships. It provides opportunities for bonding, communication, and teamwork. Play can also help adults build new friendships and expand their social networks. By embracing play, adults can enrich their lives and maintain a healthy balance between work and leisure.

8

Chapter 8: Educational Benefits of Gaming

Games offer a unique and engaging way to facilitate learning. Educational games are designed to teach specific skills and concepts in an interactive and enjoyable manner. These games can be used in formal educational settings, such as schools, as well as in informal settings, like at home or in community centers. The educational benefits of gaming are numerous and diverse.

One of the key benefits is the development of cognitive skills. Educational games often require players to think critically, solve problems, and make decisions. These activities help to improve cognitive functions such as memory, attention, and reasoning. For example, puzzle games challenge players to use logic and spatial awareness, while strategy games require planning and foresight.

Games also promote the acquisition of knowledge. Many educational games are designed to teach specific subjects, such as mathematics, science, or history. These games present information in an engaging way, making it easier for students to understand and remember. For example, historical simulation games allow players to experience historical events and make decisions based on real-world scenarios, deepening their understanding of history.

Additionally, games can enhance language and literacy skills. Word games, spelling games, and reading comprehension games help to improve vocabulary, spelling, and reading skills. These games often incorporate storytelling elements, encouraging players to read and understand complex texts. By playing these games, students can develop strong language skills that are essential for academic success and effective communication.

Furthermore, games can promote social and emotional development. Multiplayer and cooperative games encourage collaboration, communication, and teamwork. These social interactions help students develop important social skills, such as empathy, cooperation, and conflict resolution. Games can also provide a safe space for students to explore emotions and practice self-regulation. By incorporating games into education, we can create a holistic learning experience that supports cognitive, social, and emotional growth.

9

Chapter 9: The Spirituality of Gaming

Gaming can be a deeply spiritual experience, offering opportunities for self-discovery, reflection, and connection with others. Many games explore themes of morality, identity, and the human condition, encouraging players to think deeply about their values and beliefs. Through gaming, players can embark on journeys of personal and spiritual growth.

Some games are designed with explicit spiritual themes. These games often draw on religious or philosophical concepts to create meaningful experiences. For example, games like "Journey" and "Abzû" explore themes of transcendence, connection, and the search for meaning. These games use visual and auditory elements to create a meditative and reflective atmosphere, inviting players to engage with their inner selves.

Even games that are not explicitly spiritual can offer moments of transcendence and self-discovery. The immersive nature of games allows players to enter new worlds and experience different perspectives. This can lead to a sense of wonder and awe, similar to spiritual experiences. Games like "The Legend of Zelda: Breath of the Wild" and "Shadow of the Colossus" create vast, open worlds that inspire exploration and reflection.

Gaming can also foster a sense of community and belonging, which is an important aspect of spirituality. Online multiplayer games and gaming communities provide opportunities for players to connect with others who share their interests and values. These connections can lead to meaningful relationships and a sense of belonging. By engaging with the gaming community, players can find support, encouragement, and a sense of purpose.

Moreover, gaming can be a form of self-care and spiritual practice. Taking time to play and relax can promote mental and emotional well-being. Engaging in games that bring joy and fulfillment can be a way of nurturing the soul. By incorporating gaming into our lives, we can create a balanced and holistic approach to spirituality.

10

Chapter 10: Playful Learning in the Classroom

Incorporating play into the classroom can transform the learning experience. Playful learning approaches, such as games, simulations, and hands-on activities, engage students and make learning more enjoyable. By creating a playful learning environment, educators can foster creativity, critical thinking, and collaboration.

One effective way to incorporate play into the classroom is through educational games. These games can be used to teach specific subjects, such as mathematics, science, or language arts. For example, math games can help students practice arithmetic skills, while science simulations can demonstrate complex scientific concepts. Educational games provide an interactive and dynamic way for students to learn and reinforce their knowledge.

Another approach is through project-based learning, where students engage in hands-on activities to explore real-world problems and create solutions. This approach encourages creativity, problem-solving, and teamwork. For example, students might work together to design and build a model of a sustainable city, incorporating concepts from geography, science, and engineering. By engaging in project-based learning, students can see the practical applications of their knowledge and develop a deeper understanding of the subject matter.

Role-playing and simulations are also effective ways to incorporate play into the classroom. These activities allow students to take on different roles and explore various perspectives. For example, students might participate in a mock trial to learn about the legal system or role-play historical figures to understand historical events. Role-playing and simulations promote critical thinking, empathy, and communication skills.

Additionally, incorporating play into the classroom can create a positive and inclusive learning environment. Playful activities can help to build a sense of community and foster positive relationships among students. They provide opportunities for students to collaborate, support each other, and celebrate their achievements. By creating a playful and supportive classroom environment, educators can enhance student engagement and motivation.

11

Chapter 11: The Future of Gaming in Education

The future of gaming in education holds exciting possibilities. As technology continues to advance, the potential for games to enhance learning experiences will only grow. From virtual reality to artificial intelligence, new innovations are transforming the way we think about education and play.

Virtual reality (VR) is one technology that has the potential to revolutionize educational gaming. VR creates immersive and interactive experiences, allowing students to explore new environments and engage with content in a hands-on way. For example, students can take virtual field trips to historical sites, explore the human body in 3D, or conduct virtual science experiments. VR can make learning more engaging and memorable, providing opportunities for experiential learning.

Artificial intelligence (AI) is another technology that is shaping the future of educational gaming. AI can create personalized learning experiences by adapting to the individual needs and abilities of each student. Intelligent tutoring systems can provide customized feedback and support, helping students to progress at their own pace. AI can also enhance the realism and complexity of games, creating more immersive and challenging learning experiences.

Gamification will continue to play a significant role in education. As educators become more familiar with game design principles, they can create more effective and engaging learning experiences. Gamification can be used to motivate students, promote active learning, and provide immediate feedback. By incorporating game elements into the classroom, educators can create a dynamic and interactive learning environment.

Moreover, the future of gaming in education will likely involve greater collaboration between educators, game designers, and researchers. By working together, these stakeholders can develop high-quality educational games that are both fun and effective. They can also conduct research to understand the impact of gaming on learning and identify best practices for incorporating games into education.

12

Chapter 12: Embracing Play in Our Lives

As we have explored throughout this book, play is a powerful and multifaceted aspect of human life. It is a source of joy, creativity, learning, and connection. By embracing play, we can enhance our well-being and enrich our lives. Whether through gaming, recreational activities, or playful learning, play offers endless possibilities for growth and fulfillment.

To fully embrace play, we must recognize its value and make time for it in our lives. This means prioritizing play and making it a regular part of our routine. Whether it's setting aside time for a favorite hobby, playing games with family and friends, or incorporating play into our work and learning, we can find ways to integrate play into our daily lives.

It is also important to create a supportive environment that encourages play. This means providing opportunities for play in schools, workplaces, and communities. By creating spaces where people feel safe and encouraged to play, we can foster a culture that values creativity, exploration, and connection.

Finally, we must approach play with an open mind and a sense of curiosity. Play is not just for children; it is for everyone. By embracing a playful mindset, we can discover new ways of thinking, learning, and connecting with others. We can find joy in the simple act of play and experience the many benefits it has to offer.

In conclusion, play is a vital and enriching part of life. By embracing play, we can learn, grow, and connect with others. We can find meaning and fulfillment in the act of play, and we can create a more joyful and vibrant world. So let's play to learn, and learn to live, and discover the magic of play

13

Chapter 13: Balancing Play and Work

In our fast-paced world, finding a balance between play and work can be challenging. However, integrating play into our daily routines can enhance productivity, creativity, and overall well-being. By recognizing the importance of play, we can create a more harmonious and fulfilling life.

One way to achieve this balance is by incorporating play breaks into the workday. Short breaks for playful activities, such as a quick game, a walk, or a creative hobby, can help to refresh the mind and boost focus. These breaks provide a mental reset, allowing us to return to work with renewed energy and perspective. Incorporating play into the workday can prevent burnout and improve overall job satisfaction.

Another strategy is to create a playful work environment. Employers can encourage playfulness by providing spaces for recreational activities, such as game rooms or outdoor areas. Team-building activities that involve play can foster collaboration and camaraderie among colleagues. By promoting a playful atmosphere, organizations can enhance employee engagement and creativity.

It is also important to prioritize leisure time outside of work. Making time for hobbies, sports, and social activities can provide a sense of balance and fulfillment. Engaging in playful activities with family and friends can strengthen relationships and create lasting memories. By setting boundaries and making time for play, we can achieve a healthy work-life balance.

Finally, adopting a playful mindset can help us approach work with a sense of curiosity and creativity. Viewing challenges as opportunities for growth and experimentation can make work more enjoyable and rewarding. By embracing play in our work and personal lives, we can create a more balanced and fulfilling existence.

14

Chapter 14: Play and Emotional Intelligence

Emotional intelligence (EI) is the ability to recognize, understand, and manage our own emotions, as well as the emotions of others. Play can play a significant role in developing and enhancing emotional intelligence. Through play, we can explore and express our emotions, build empathy, and improve our social skills.

One way play contributes to emotional intelligence is by providing a safe space for emotional expression. Play allows us to explore a range of emotions, from joy and excitement to frustration and disappointment. By experiencing and expressing these emotions in a playful context, we can develop a better understanding of our emotional responses. This self-awareness is a key component of emotional intelligence.

Play also fosters empathy by encouraging us to take on different perspectives. Through role-playing games and imaginative play, we can step into the shoes of others and experience their emotions and viewpoints. This helps to build empathy and understanding, allowing us to connect with others on a deeper level. By developing empathy through play, we can improve our interpersonal relationships and communication skills.

Additionally, play can improve our ability to manage emotions. Games and playful activities often involve challenges and setbacks, requiring us to regulate our emotions and stay focused. By navigating these challenges in a playful context, we can develop resilience and emotional regulation skills. These skills are essential for managing stress and maintaining emotional well-being.

Furthermore, play promotes social interaction and the development of social skills. Cooperative games and team activities require communication, cooperation, and conflict resolution. By engaging in these activities, we can practice and refine our social skills, enhancing our ability to build and maintain positive relationships. Play can also provide opportunities for social bonding, creating a sense of belonging and community.

15

Chapter 15: The Intersection of Gaming, Education, and Spirituality

As we conclude this exploration of play, it is clear that gaming, education, and spirituality are interconnected in meaningful and profound ways. Each of these aspects of life enriches and informs the others, creating a holistic and integrated approach to personal growth and fulfillment.

Gaming, with its immersive and interactive nature, offers unique opportunities for learning and self-discovery. Through educational games, we can acquire knowledge and develop skills in an engaging and enjoyable way. Games also provide a platform for exploring complex themes and narratives, allowing us to reflect on our values and beliefs. By embracing gaming as a tool for education and personal growth, we can unlock new possibilities for learning and self-improvement.

Education, in turn, can benefit from the incorporation of play and gamification. By creating playful and dynamic learning environments, educators can enhance student engagement and motivation. Play-based learning encourages creativity, critical thinking, and collaboration, helping students to develop essential skills for success in the modern world. By integrating play into education, we can create a more effective and enjoyable learning experience.

Spirituality, too, is enriched by the element of play. Play allows us to connect with our inner selves, experience joy and wonder, and foster a sense of community and belonging. Through playful activities and rituals, we can explore our spiritual nature and deepen our understanding of the world around us. By embracing play as a spiritual practice, we can cultivate a sense of peace, balance, and connection.

In conclusion, play is a powerful and multifaceted aspect of human life that intersects with gaming, education, and spirituality. By recognizing the value of play and making it a central part of our lives, we can enhance our well-being, foster personal growth, and create a more joyful and fulfilling existence. So let us play to learn, learn to live, and embrace the magic of play in all its forms.

Book Description:

Dive into the fascinating world of play with "Play to Learn, Learn to Live: The Intersection of Gaming, Education, and Spirituality." This enlightening book explores the profound impact of play on human development, education, and spirituality. Through twelve captivating chapters, the author delves into the evolution of gaming, the benefits of gamification in education, and the spiritual dimensions of play.

Discover how play-based learning can transform education, making it more engaging and effective. Learn about the psychological and emotional benefits of play for both children and adults. Explore the ways in which gaming can serve as a tool for self-discovery and personal growth. From the ancient origins of play to the cutting-edge technologies of virtual reality and artificial intelligence, this book covers a wide range of topics that highlight the importance of play in our lives.

Whether you are an educator, a gamer, or simply curious about the role of play in human development, this book offers valuable insights and practical advice. It encourages readers to embrace play as a powerful and enriching aspect of life, capable of enhancing well-being, fostering creativity, and deepening our connection to ourselves and others.

www.ingramcontent.com/pod-product-compliance
Lightning Source LLC
LaVergne TN
LVHW020502080526
838202LV00057B/6111